T0087406

# TOUCH THE SPIRIT

*for*

## TRUMPET

*and*

## ORCHESTRA

MUSIC MINUS ONE

6839

6839

# CONTENTS

> High-register notes throughout this album may be performed
> *8vb* where this is more comfortable for the player.

## *SUGGESTIONS FOR USING THIS MMO EDITION*

WE HAVE TRIED to create a product that will provide you an easy way to learn and perform these arias with a full orchestra in the comfort of your own home. The following MMO features and techniques will reduce these inflexibilities and help you maximize the effectiveness of the MMO practice and performance system:

Because it involves a fixed orchestral performance, there is an inherent lack of flexibility in tempo and cadenza length. We have observed generally accepted tempi, and always in the originally intended key, but some may wish to perform at a different tempo, or to slow down or speed up the accompaniment for practice purposes; or to alter the piece to a more comfortable key. You can purchase from MMO specialized CD players & recorders which allow variable speed while maintaining proper pitch, and vice versa. This is an indispensable tool for the serious musician and you may wish to look into purchasing this useful piece of equipment for full enjoyment of all your MMO editions.

We want to provide you with the most useful practice and performance accompaniments possible. If you have any suggestions for improving the MMO system, please feel free to contact us. You can reach us by e-mail at *info@musicminusone.com*.

## FOREWORD

Each tune in *Touch the Spirit* has been re-harmonized, arranged and performed by me and then sequenced for symphony orchestra. I'm sure you will agree that the orchestration and sequencing of each track is of exceptional quality. As you can hear on the recordings, these melodies require an extreme upper register for trumpet. When performing them, my goal is to not just play the high notes, but to keep an open sound regardless of how high the melody ascends into the upper register. In addition to listening to the obvious great high-note trumpet players, I suggest listening to the three tenors, Carreras, Domingo and Pavarotti as an example of correct breath-control and body posturing for producing an open sound, especially in the upper register.

I would be interested in hearing you perform any of these tunes. If you have the opportunity to make a recording please send me a CD, or email me an MP3 file of your performance. <wnaus@berklee.edu>

Thanks again and enjoy the music!!

—*Wayne Naus*

4

# "Amazing Grace"

Comp. J Newton
Arr. Naus

MMO 6839

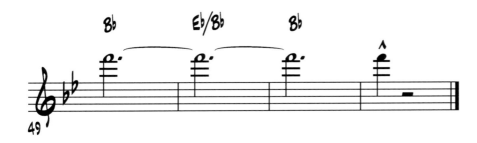

# "Star Spangled Banner"

Comp. F.S. Key
Arr. W. Naus

MMO 6839

# "America the Beautiful"

Bb

Comp. K.L.Bates
Arr. W.Naus

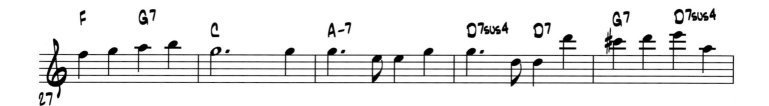

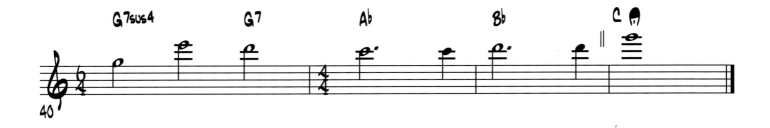

Bb

# "The Lord's Prayer"

Traditional
Arr. Naus

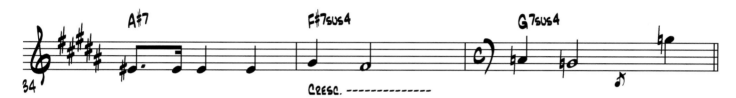

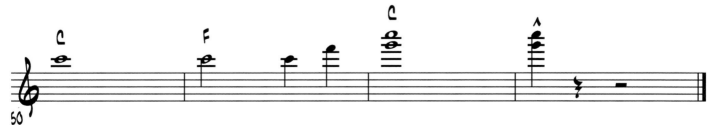

# "God Bless America"

Comp. Irviong Berlin
Arr. Naus

Bb

# "Flying Without Wings"

Comp. S.Mac/W.Hector
Arr.W.Naus

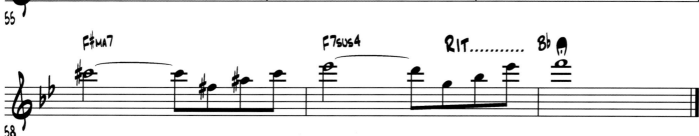

# "Taps"

Bb

Recording featuring spoken word performance by Mr. Carl Beane

O.W. Norton
Arr. W. Naus

**MMO Music Group, Inc.**
**50 Executive Boulevard - Elmsford, NY 10523**
**1.800.669.7464 (USA) - 1.914.592.1188 (Int'l)**
**www.musicminusone.com**